Supervisor's Guide
Lean and
Performance Driven

Revision 5

Eric M. Gatmaitan

About the Author

Eric M. Gatmaitan earned a master of business administration degree with emphasis on business information systems from Western Michigan University and a bachelor of science degree in industrial management engineering with a minor in mechanical engineering from De La Salle University.

Mr. Gatmaitan is the author of *Manager's Guide to Lean and Performance*, *Building a Citadel*, and *Beginner's Guide to Crystal Reports 2013*. He is a former faculty member at Western Michigan University, where he taught computer technology application and programming.

In the construction and manufacturing industries, he served as an industrial engineer, production supervisor, plant manager, and chief operating officer.

As a consultant, Mr. Gatmaitan leads projects and conducts training in the areas of strategic planning, business process optimization, quality systems, and performance management systems.

Ant Illustration: Paul Sizer, Sizer Design + Illustration More info at www.paulsizer.com

Table of Contents

Table of Contents

Table of Contents

Introduction

The goal of a supervisor is to deliver goods and services that meet an organization's established performance standards for safety, quality, delivery, and cost. Achieving the performance standards requires a supervisor to go beyond managing people. It extends to managing *all* resources such as people, equipment, materials, methods, and data. The role of a supervisor is to manage a system with interrelated elements that need to work together toward a common goal.

I initially developed the methods in this book during my days as a production supervisor for a medical-device manufacturing company. The successful implementation of these methods help elevated my role to a division manager. For more than twenty-five years, as an industrial engineer and management consultant, I continued to use the methods in this book, further improving and validating their effectiveness at enhancing organizational performance.

This book outlines the fundamental structure necessary to establish and manage an effective workforce. The step-by-step guide found at the end of each chapter is a compilation of processes implemented at various industries, from small mom-and-pop businesses to large Fortune 100 companies. Process-improvement tools used in initiatives such as Lean Six Sigma, Total Quality Management, and the Toyota Production System are most effective, and long lasting, when the fundamental structure in this book is implemented.

In my first supervisory job, a production team was working ten hours a day Monday through Saturday and half a day on Sunday. Product demand was growing, and the production team built up inventory for thirty-one days, yet back orders were a major customer service issue.

In response, we developed a management support-staff and team structure focused on achieving key performance measures. Within the first four weeks of launching the structured organizational process, performance data guided operational teams to implement small-lot production, balancing production requirements to specific product demands. Production hours were scaled back to regular hours, and work order quantities were cut by 50 percent. This enabled us to reduce product inventory to a nine-day supply and reduce back orders by 75 percent, significantly improving customer service.

This book illustrates the process used to impact performance measures.

Chapter 1 outlines the structure of and methods for establishing an operational-level team environment. It also provides methods for supervisors to manage day-to-day activities through a team structure.

Long-term viability of a team structure hinges on a support staff monitoring operational team performance and providing technical assistance. In chapter 2, the support staff structure is presented to allow an organization to gather operational performance data and swiftly address issues that slow down or stops work teams from achieving their objectives.

Crucial to the work-team and support-staff structure is an organizational focus on process compliance throughout the entire supply chain. Chapter 3 examines the requirements of people, machines, materials, methods, and data to achieve total-system compliance.

Maintaining and improving compliance requires vigilance at identifying symptomatic issues that lead to nonconformances and the implementation of incremental improvements.

Chapter 4 presents a simple but robust process of issue resolution and employee suggestion that will enable employees to eliminate issues proactively and participate in continuous improvement efforts. An open and robust process improvement system is detailed in chapter 4. When implemented properly, you can expect rapid improvements impacting performance outcomes. I have seen numerous organizations with work teams consistently implementing two process improvements per person per month, or two hundred process improvements per month in an organization with one hundred people.

Chapter 5 outlines the process for implementing the Five Basics of Workplace Organization, also known as 5S. This chapter includes an audit checklist to help kick off an organizational standard for workplace organization in both office and manufacturing environments. Amazingly, I have seen companies implement the process in chapter 5 effectively and reduce inventory by 35 percent within a month.

An easy-to-use, data-driven, and objective performance-review system provides a mechanism to motivate employees to participate fully in a performance-driven work environment. Chapter 6 presents a job performance review (JPR) system that is supervisor and employee friendly. During the implementation process, supervisors should maintain focus on the desired operational outcome of the concepts of *lean and performance*. Across all industries, *lean* refers to the efficient use of people, machines, materials, methods, and data. Eliminating waste and streamlining the operation is a constant pursuit. A set of key performance measures balances the outcomes of safety, quality, delivery, and cost. This enables a high-perfomance team to function independently, apply corrective action, and continually improve the process. As a plant manager for a medical device company, I witnessed a fully coordinated workforce with minimal gray areas on objectives and goals. Everyone was data driven, objective, process compliant, and customer focused.

With a structured process and successful implementation, an organization can realize significant productivity gains and improve employee morale.

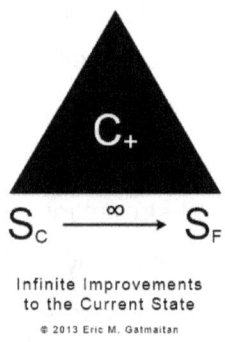

Infinite Improvements
to the Current State

© 2013 Eric M. Gatmaitan

Chapter 1: Developing Self-Sufficiency

Manage Operations through Work Teams

Supervisors must position themselves at a vantage point viewing the bigger picture of the business system or manufacturing system. This will maximize the supervisor's influence on overall performance. Managing forty people in a department can be a chore, but managing five team leaders is so much easier.

Work teams can be formed as either functional teams or product-service teams. A functional team is a natural grouping of people performing similar tasks or functions. A product-service team has a clear objective of building products or providing a service. Often, this type of work team is more diverse and is spread throughout the building.

If people are spread out in a large area where one or two people work at a work center, it may be difficult to group people into work teams. Try the steps below to define work teams.

1. Draw a flow diagram of the process.

2. Identify segments in the process, either by function, subassembly, or machine centers.

3. Identify the number of people in each segment.

4. Group people in teams of no more than eight members. Teams of more than eight will demand more oversight and structure.

The Supervisor Providing Technical Support

Supervisors experience a big role change when teams are formed. They begin to focus more on setting goals and letting teams operate autonomously. The supervisor's roles in a team environment are to monitor system roadblocks, provide resources, and continuously strive to improve the team's overall performance.

The change in the supervisor's role provides big benefits to both the supervisor and the entire organization. Imagine every element in the system delivered on time and performing as expected. This situation eliminates the firefighting mode that most supervisors seem to assume in response to normal, day-to-day occurrences.

The first two hours of a work shift is the most critical time of the day. It sets the tone for the day, whether good or bad. An all-out effort should be made to set a positive tone by having the supervisors and the technical-support staff assure all elements are working together. No meetings should be scheduled during this critical time frame.

Process Compliance

The primary role and function of a team member is process compliance. Process stability and predictability make it easy to resolve issues. Problems become unnecessarily complex if there is no set pattern to identify root causes and apply an effective corrective action.

Supervisors must remind team members that their job is *not* to make a product or provide a service. Their job is to perform the standard process and ensure products and services are delivered with the highest levels of efficiency, quality, and customer satisfaction.

A Common Goal Builds Teamwork

Organizing a team is the easy part. Self-sufficiency of a team comes with these steps:

1. Identify a set of performance objectives.

2. Define the roles and responsibilities of each member.

3. Train and coach each person to perform his or her tasks.

4. Observe team members to collect performance data.

5. Present performance feedback.

6. Provide resources and guidance to improve the process.

The Common Goal

Identifying key performance measures is similar to building an instrument panel that indicates the status of the suppliers, team, and customers throughout the entire process.

A process goes through input, process, and output phases. In the input phase, suppliers provide all of the resources for the team to function. Next, the work team performs the process using equipment and methods. In the output phase, customers receive the products and services produced by a work team.

Within each phase are broad goal categories of safety, quality, delivery, cost, and continuous improvement.

The safety category monitors workplace injuries, accidents, near misses, and lost time. Quality looks at process compliance with customer specifications, including dimensional specifications and items that can't be measured objectively, such as cosmetic requirements. The delivery category measures how well an organization complies with customer specified delivery times, quantities, and quality conformance. A continuous improvement category monitors the continuing efforts to improve existing systems and procedures, such as suggestions, procedure writing, training, and system audits.

Below is a planning matrix for identifying potential performance measures. It blends the input-process-output process and the categories of safety, quality, delivery, and cost.

	Input (supplier)	Process (team)	Output (finished product)
Safety	Hazardous material leaks	Accidents and near misses	Stack height compliance
Quality	Defects received	Defects produced	Defects shipped
Delivery	On-time delivery	Schedule compliance	On-time delivery
Cost	Purchase-price variance	Productivity	Purchase-price variance
Continuous Improvement	NCR-CAR	NCR-CAR suggestions	NCR-CAR

As you begin to develop your own matrix, list as many performance measures as you can. Then select six to eight key performance measures.

Providing Performance Feedback

Key performance measures must be easy to gather, present, and understand. Charting is an effective method of presenting data to a team. In most cases, a manually drawn chart is more practical and easier to manage than a computer-generated chart.

Every chart must indicate the performance objective or expectation. On the first set of charts, use the historical average as the standard or goal. The standards should clearly indicate the common goal and easily communicate whether performance is below or above the expected level.

Coach the team to ask continually, "What made us perform below or above the expected level?" Obviously, we all want to avoid unfavorable performance. In cases when performance exceeds the goal, we need to also ask, "How can we continue to perform above the goal line?"

Delegating Team Leadership

The organization will have to coach the supervisor to examine the business system and manage the department through team leaders and team representatives.

A team can be manged by a team leader or a team representative. A team leader is one level higher than the members of a team and is a permanent job position. Team representative, on the other hand, is a temporary assignment to a team member, for a period of at least three months. Both options can work effectively.

A team leader should have an assigned backup person to ensure process continuity when the he or she is not available.

If your organization chooses the team representative option, a team member should be assigned for onboarding or training. Soon after assigning a team representative, the former team representatives can be assigned the backup role.

Moving forward, the terms *team representative* and *team leader* will be used interchangeably.

Selecting a Team Leader

A team leader must be able to motivate a team to focus on the process and strive to meet objectives. Leadership qualities are needed at the introduction of the team structure. As the process matures, the team-leadership role shifts from being person dependent to process dependent.

Initially, the supervisor should take the team leader role for the first six to eight weeks. During this time, he or she can monitor the process and make adjustments to fit the department's needs. This is also the best time to train and coach the team leader.

Role of the Team Leader

The team leader will perform the following tasks:

- Collect and review performance data.
- Make sure every member actively participates in team meetings and activities.
- Provide an objective assessment of performance outcomes.
- Align team focus with goals and objectives.
- Coordinate feedback for suggestions, concerns, and issues.

Routine Performance Review

A meeting area should be set up as the communications center, and a bulletin board should be installed to display vacation plans, performance indicators, production schedules, and other information to help the team plan and achieve its goals. The meeting area must be close to the work area. Noise level and lighting should be considered to ensure that an effective meeting can be conducted there.

Guided by an agenda and procedure, the team leader should conduct each meeting on time and within a fifteen-minute time limit. Ideally, meetings should be scheduled at the start of a shift to set the tone for the day. The agenda will routinely cover the following items:

1. Staffing and vacation plan
2. The previous day's performance
3. Plan for the day
4. Critical materials
5. Concerns, issues, and suggestions

The team leader should coordinate the identification of issues that slow down the team or stop it from achieving its goals. All issues should then be validated by the team, and a proposed corrective action should be developed and implemented.

Long problem-solving sessions are to be scheduled outside the routine team meetings. Only quick problem-solving activities should be discussed in the fifteen-minute team meeting.

Resolution of issues will occur mainly at the team level. However, issues that require technical support and additional resources should be directed to the support staff.

Developing Self-Sufficiency

Step-by-Step Procedures
Developing Self-Sufficiency

Creating the Team Structure

Instructions

1. Define the team's purpose and objectives.

2. Select a team name.

3. Schedule the routine team meeting. For the operations staff, a daily performance review scheduled at the start of the shift is recommended because the meeting sets the tone for the rest of the shift.

4. List team members. This will be their home team. They may work temporarily in other departments, but this is where they will attend the daily meetings.

5. Define the team leader's roles and duties of the team leader.

6. Select the team leader.

7. Select the backup team leader.

8. Create a roster of employees.

9. Route the team roster to all department employees and managers for feedback and approval.

Identifying Performance Measures

Instructions

1. Identify the customers and suppliers.

2. Use the planning matrix to identify potential performance measures.

	Input (supplier)	Process (team)	Output (finished product)
Safety	Hazardous material leaks	Accidents and near misses	Stack height compliance
Quality	Defects received	Defects produced	Defects shipped
Delivery	On-time delivery	Schedule compliance	On-time delivery
Cost	Purchase-price variance	Productivity	Purchase-price variance
Continuous Improvement	NCR-CAR	NCR-CAR Suggestions 5S score	NCR-CAR

3. Choose no more than eight measurements that represent the team's overall performance.

4. Add scorecards for issue resolution and suggestions.

5. Define each performance measure and sources of data.

6. Route the data definitions to the next-level manager for feedback and approval.

7. Continually review relevance of performance measures.

Collecting Performance Data

Instructions

1. Develop a simple data-collection process for new key performance measures. When possible, the team should collect the data. This will increase ownership of performance data and decrease dependence on the support staff.

2. Create data-collection forms, if necessary.

3. Designate a central location for team members to submit data-collection forms.

4. Create a tally sheet or spreadsheet on which the team leader can compile the data.

5. Write a detailed procedure for how to collect and tally the data using the forms.

6. Train the team on the data-collection process.

7. For two weeks, test the data-collection process for accuracy and timeliness.

8. Improve the data-collection process, if necessary.

9. Integrate the data-collection process into the daily work routine.

Setting Up the Meeting Area

Instructions

1. Purchase a board (a four-by-eight pinboard works well). Additional boards may be needed as the team progresses at using visual management tools.

2. Select a meeting area large enough for the team board and team members. Ensure that a clock can be seen from the meeting area.

3. Organize and clean the meeting area. Remove unnecessary items or postings. Ensure that the area is well lit and quiet enough for a meeting.

4. Mount the pinboard on the wall or on a movable stand.

5. Mark and label the area with the team name. Mark it with floor tape if in a production area.

6. Post team information such as calendars, production and staffing schedules, pictures of team members, and so on.

7. Post temporary notices, indicating the expiration date in the corner of each.

Displaying Performance Data

Instructions

1. Choose a time frame for each performance item (daily, weekly, or monthly).

2. Choose a chart type for each measurement (bar, line, stacked bar, combination, or custom).

3. Standardize the use of color, such as green for actual values and a black line for the goal.

4. Create a chart template for each performance measure.

5. Copy charts onto cardstock to keep the markers from bleeding onto the pinboard and to prevent paper warping due to humidity changes.

6. Write the team name, time period, and legend on each chart.

7. Label the chart index, making sure the data average is about 75 percent of the total chart height.

8. Chart the performance data. Be sure to write in the value of any data point that goes beyond the top of the scale. Do not draw above the charting boundary.

Example Daily Chart

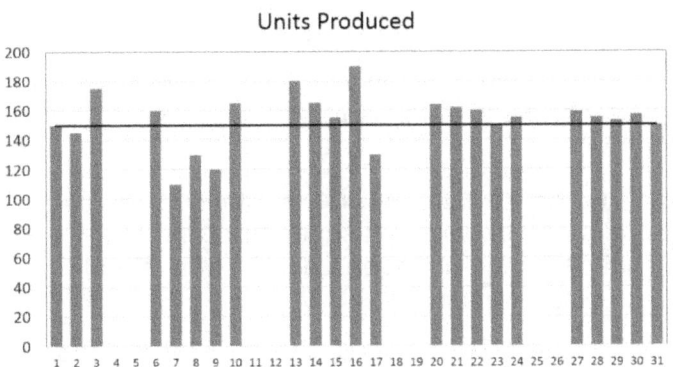

Example Monthly Chart

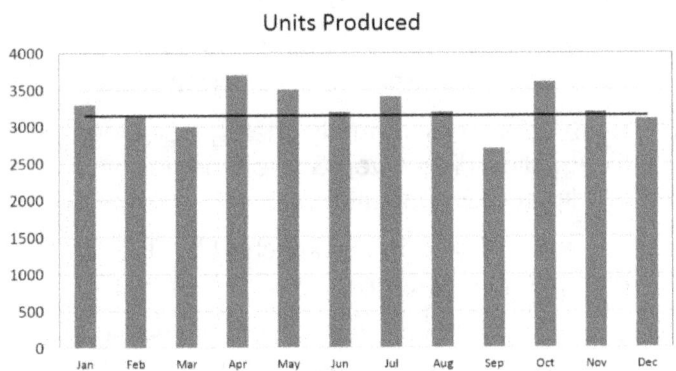

Setting Performance Goals

Instructions

1. Gather and examine historical data.

2. Schedule a meeting with the team leaders, department supervisor, and department manager.

3. Inspect the monthly charts with the team leaders, department supervisor, and department manager. Look for trends and relationships.

4. Calculate the historical average of each chart. Reference the team's tally sheet.

5. Set goals to match company objectives.

6. Determine the impact of these goals on financial, operational, and company goals. Link the monthly goals to budgets, staffing levels, capacity, and production objectives.

7. Create a formal action plan for any goal that is significantly different from its current value.

8. Set a goal for all monthly charts, including Suggestions Received & Implemented and Workplace Organization.

9. Set a goal for each weekly chart by dividing the monthly goal by four.

10. Set a goal for each daily chart by dividing the monthly goal by the average number of days worked.

11. Mark the performance goal on the chart with a black horizontal line. The line should span the entire width of the chart. Use colored lines if there are multiple goals on one chart.

12. Write the exact value of each goal on its axis.

13. Record the goals on the agenda.

14. Explain to the team that performance planning takes practice and patience and that the goals will become more accurate and meaningful as the team gains experience using them.

15. During team meetings, discuss differences between the actual data and the goals.

Developing the Meeting Agenda

Instructions

1. Design a section for each of the following:
   a. Staffing and attendance
   b. Performance review
   c. Plan for the day
   d. Follow-up list for critical materials or supplies
   e. Unplanned events
   f. Follow-up list for issues and concerns
   g. Status of suggestions
2. Customize the agenda to include specific team needs.
3. Limit the agenda to two pages so it can be printed on one double-sided agenda form.

Conducting a Team Meeting

Instructions

1. Go to the meeting area about five minutes before the scheduled meeting.

2. Review the agenda for accuracy and completeness.

3. Position yourself on the left side of the team board.

4. Coach members to form a single-layer semicircle around the team board as they come into the meeting area.

5. Start the meeting on time by greeting the team with a standard greeting, such as "Welcome, everyone" or "Good morning. Let us start."

6. Look around to review attendance, and note any unplanned absence or tardiness. Identify members who are on planned vacations, on reassignments, or in training.

7. Ask the team for updates on upcoming staffing plans, such as vacations, training, or reassignments.

8. Review each performance measure by pointing to the chart. Read the actual value, and compare it to the goal (standard or expected value). Mention whether it is under, on, or over the goal.

9. Ask team members for their feedback when the actual performance value is significantly different from the goal.

10. Determine whether the feedback given by the team needs to be listed in the issues log.

11. Ask team members for any issues with supplies or materials that require attention, including resupply.

12. Ask about any general concerns and issues.

13. Get agreement from the team regarding whether a particular issue is valid for the log sheet.

14. Review the status of issues on the log sheet.

15. Review any new suggestions issued, and determine whether each suggestion is valid. Get agreement from the team to pursue implementation, and document the suggestion on the log sheet for implementation.

16. Before ending the meeting, ask "Are there any other concerns or issues?"

17. End the meeting with a decisive statement, such as, "This ends our team meeting. Have a great day!"

Chapter 2: Building the Support Structure

The Technical-Support Staff

Maintaining an operation to focus on peorcess and performance standards requires a support structure to help operational teams resolve issues beyond their scope of responsibility and authority.

The technical support staff is typically led by the department supervisor and complemented by a group of specialists in areas such as quality, purchasing, engineering, and maintenance. Leading the agenda are team leaders presenting performance outcomes, relaying operational issues, and recommending a corrective action plan. The supervisor provides leadership by coordinating and ensuring swift completion of corrective actions.

A conference room is typically the designated meeting area for the support staff. Some companies post performance charts on the wall to represent each work team. This makes deviations from the standards easy to identify, with each chart showing the latest team data and the expected level of performance.

The diagram below shows the big-picture view of the team and technical-support structure. Multiple support-staff levels may be deployed; this choice is dictated by the size of the organization.

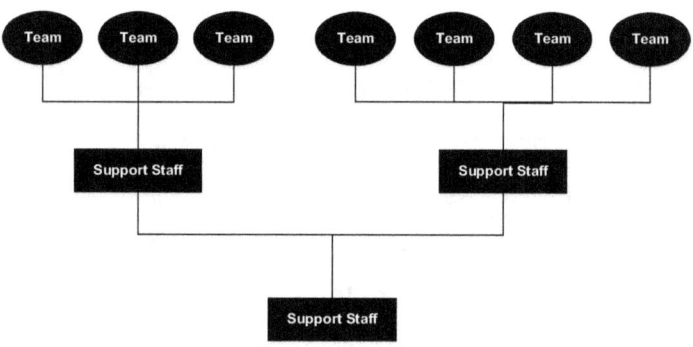

The structure is essentially an upside-down organizational chart. This organizational approach focuses on the needs of the operational teams and ensures conformance to customer requirements. This bottom-up reporting of performance provides quick feedback on the effectiveness of a company's strategy.

Performance Measures

The performance measures of the technical support staff include the consolidated performance of the work teams. Performance metrics for support-staff effectiveness include the following:

- Issues (received, addressed, oldest open)
- Suggestions (received, implemented, oldest open)
- Nonconformances (received, corrective actions completed, oldest open)

Presenting Performance Data

Presenting from hand drawn charts posted on the wall may appear technologically backward compared to using computer-generated charts and an overhead projector. However, hand-drawn charts are simple and easy to update before each meeting.

Decide wisely between hand-drawn charts and computer-generated charts. Keep the objective in mind, and use charts to communicate data the quickest and easiest way.

Whatever charting method is used, the supervisor must not be tempted to take over the collection of data and charting of team performance. The entire team must have ownership of the performance data to gain autonomy and self-sufficiency.

The Support-Staff Meeting

The routine support-staff meeting is scheduled based on the data cycle. Often, meaningful data requires a few days or a week. Thus, meeting frequency can range from daily to weekly.

Below is an example of an agenda:

1. Each team
    a. Performance review
    b. New issues and concerns
    c. Follow-up on issues and oncerns
2. Action items
    a. New items
    b. Review of open items
3. Support staff performance metrics review

The meeting should start promptly and conclude within thirty minutes. Problem-solving activities should be scheduled separately. A roster of backup meeting facilitators should be defined to ensure that the meeting proceeds as scheduled.

Building the Support Structure

Step-by-Step Procedures
Building the Support Structure

Creating the Support-Staff Structure

Instructions

1. Choose a standard meeting frequency. The meeting should be scheduled to begin two hours after the start of the shift.

2. Identify the support-staff members, including the leaders of the work teams.

3. Define the role and duties of the support-staff team leader.

4. Choose the initial backup team leader, and create a list of succeeding backup leaders.

5. Create a support-staff roster. Use function titles instead of employee names, such as assembly team leader, engineering specialist, and manufacturing manager.

6. Route the support-staff roster to all department employees and managers for feedback and approval.

Identifying Performance Measures

Instructions

Operational Team Review

1. Identify team performance measures for the support staff to review.

2. Identify performance measures for each support-staff function, if needed.

Department Review

1. Identify the department's customers and suppliers.

2. Use the performance-measure planning matrix below.

	Input (supplier)	Process (team)	Output (customer)
Safety	Hazardous material leaks	Accidents and near misses	Stack height compliance
Quality	Defects received	Defects produced	Defects shipped
Delivery	On-time delivery	Schedule compliance	On-time delivery
Cost	Purchase-price variance	Productivity	Purchase-price variance
Continuous Improvement	NCR-CAR	NCR-CAR suggestions 5S score	NCR-CAR

3. Choose a maximum of eight measurements that represent the team's overall performance.

4. Add scorecards for the issue-resolution process and suggestion system.

5. Define each performance measure and sources of data.

6. Route the data definitions to all department employees and managers for feedback and approval.

7. Review key performance measures annually, and update if necessary.

Presenting Performance Measures

Instructions

1. Select a charting time frame (weekly or monthly).

2. Map out a chart for each operational team and support-staff function.

3. Lay out the charts for the department.

4. Choose a chart type for each measurement (bar, line, stacked bar, combination, or custom).

5. Choose colors for each key measurement.

6. Create a chart template for each performance measure.

7. Copy charts onto cardstock to keep the markers from bleeding onto the pinboard and to prevent paper warping due to humidity changes.

8. Write the index on each chart by hand with a dark pen. The data should average about 60 percent of the total chart height.

9. Chart the data with a ruler. Use the narrow tip of a marker for daily bars and the wide tip for monthly bars.

10. Write in the value of any data point that goes off the top of the scale. Do not draw above the charting boundary.

11. Describe unusual highs or lows by placing a note near the data point.

Setting Goals

Instructions

1. Collect data for at least six weeks.

2. Schedule a meeting with the team leader, department supervisor, and department manager. Meet in the team area.

3. Inspect the monthly charts (January through December) during the meeting with the team leader, department supervisor, and department manager. Meet in the team area.

   - Look for trends and relationships between current and past data.
   - Look for trends and relationships among different charts.
   - Calculate the historical average of each performance measure.

4. Set goals to match company objectives. Consider the effects of fiscal-year and calendar-year objectives.

5. Determine the impact of these goals on financial, operational, and company goals.

6. Link monthly goals to financial budgets, staffing levels, capacity, and production objectives.

7. Create a formal action plan for each goal that is significantly different from its current value.

8. Set a goal for all monthly charts, including Suggestions Received & Implemented and Workplace Organization.

9. Set a goal for every weekly chart by dividing the monthly goal by four.

10. Set a goal for each daily chart by dividing the monthly goal by the average number of workdays.

11. Indicate performance goals with a black horizontal line. The line should span the entire width of the chart. Use a ruler. Use colored lines if there are multiple goals.

12. Write the exact value of each goal.

13. Record the goals on a blank meeting agenda. Make copies from this master until the goals change.

14. Explain to the team that performance planning takes practice and patience and that the goals will become more accurate and meaningful as the team gains experience with team performance reviews.

15. Discuss any differences between the actual data and the goals during the team meetings.

Establishing the Meeting Area

Instructions

1.   Secure a meeting area.

2.   Organize and clean the room as necessary. Remove unnecessary furniture or postings. Silence telephones so they won't ring during the meeting.

3.   Mount a pinboard to post performance metrics. Start with one four-by-eight-inch board, and add custom sizes to cover as much wall area as needed.

4.   Mount a dry-erase board, a projection screen, and a clock to monitor the length of meeting.

5.   Post the name of the support-staff team on the board.

6.   Post support-staff information, such as calendars, production schedules, and staffing plans.

7.   Post general notices. Indicate the expiration date in the corner of each temporary notice.

Developing the Meeting Agenda

Instructions

1. Design an agenda section to discuss staffing and attendance with each team.

2. Design an agenda section to review yesterday's performance as indicated by each team's key performance measures.

3. Design an agenda section to discuss each team's plan for the day.

4. Design an agenda section to record and follow up on each team's critical material or supply issues. Include a "Done" column to indicate which issues have been resolved.

5. Design an agenda section to discuss each team's unplanned events.

6. Design an agenda section to record and follow up on each team's issues and concerns. Include a "Done" column to indicate which issues have been resolved.

7. Design the agenda so that each team discusses all of their sections before proceeding to the next team.

8. Add a section for support functions next on the agenda, such as Engineering and Purchasing topics. Design an agenda section to discuss suggestions if necessary.

9. Add a general announcements section at the end of the agenda.

Conducting a Support-Staff Meeting

Instructions

1.   Start the meeting on time. Do not wait for late members.

2.   Discuss any staffing issues with the first team leader indicated on the agenda.

3.   Request the previous day's performance measures from the first team leader.

4.   Request the previous week's totals and month-to-date numbers on the first day of each week.

5.   Request the previous month's totals on the first day of each month.

6.   Ask the team leader why the data are unusually good or bad. Ask other support-staff members to get them involved.

7.   Record the performance measures on the agenda with supporting notes.

8.   Examine the charts to spot trends or relationships.

9.   Discuss any differences between actual performance and expected outcomes.

10. Discuss the plan for the day with the first team leader. Discuss scheduling priorities as necessary.

11. Record a brief summary of the plan for the day for the first team.

12. Ask for any new critical issues with raw materials or supplies.

13. Record issues for follow-up. Identify specific items and when they are needed.

14. Discuss the status of any open issues with raw materials or supplies. Follow up on delegated action plans.

15. Check off any issues that have been resolved since the last meeting in the Done column of the agenda.

16. Ask if about any unplanned events since the last meeting. This brief discussion will bring out issues and concerns.

17. Ask for any new issues or concerns. Let the team leader explain the concern for about one minute. If his or her explanation exceeds one minute, explain to all that this discussion must be brief and to the point.

18. Summarize the issue, and then ask if the issue was summarized correctly. Clarify if necessary.

19. Record the issue for follow-up. This reassures the team leader that it will not be forgotten or ignored. Start follow-up items with an action verb.

20. Inform the team members when feedback will be provided. The more important the issue, the quicker the response should be, often by the next support-staff meeting.

21. Delegate follow-up action plans to support-staff members.

22. Discuss the status of any open issues or concerns. Follow up on delegated action plans.

23. In the Done column of the agenda, check off any issues that have been resolved since the last meeting.

24. Delegate problem-solving discussions to the appropriate people. Problem-solving sessions should be scheduled separately.

25. Reschedule sensitive issues. Take time to prepare for the discussion of such issues by validating facts or requesting support from other managers or departments. Encourage guest speakers to attend.

26. Discuss the status of any open projects involving this team. Keep it brief.

27. Ask the team leader for any brief announcements.

28. Repeat discussion of staffing, performance, the plan for the following day, and issues with each team leader.

29. Discuss support-function topics, such as engineering or purchasing issues.

30. Discuss the status of suggestions briefly with the entire support staff.

31. End the meeting on a positive note. Coach the support staff to complete the meeting in twenty to thirty minutes.

Chapter 3: Focus on Compliance

It is difficult to improve a system with inconsistencies spread all over the place. Inconsistencies in following procedures or deviations to performance standards are also known as nonconformances.

Types of nonconformances include people not following set policies and procedures, machines not being properly maintained or set up, raw materials mixed with defective items, procedures that are impractical, and incomplete data.

Focusing on system compliance establishes the foundation for long-term process improvements. System compliance leads to process stability and predictability, and It is much easier to troubleshoot an issue in a stable and predictable environment.

Below are the system elements and basic resources needed to build system compliance.

Elements	Basic Resource Needs
People	• Baseline qualifications • Training and coaching • Performance objectives and feedback
Machines	• Validation of equipment capabilities • Maintenance schedule • Setup procedures • Operating specifications
Materials	• Material and delivery specifications • Quality assurance inspection protocols
Methods	• Policy and procedures • Guidelines
Data	• Product and/or service specifications • Records

People

Jobs must be appropriately assigned to individuals who have the basic skills and training to perform the required task. Supervisors should keep in mind that *common sense* is a broad term and that there are no books of standards when it comes to common sense.

Training

The best opportunity for an organization to establish a consistent process is during initial training. Effective training involves two distinct parts: (1) the trainer demonstrating the process and (2) the trainee performing the process from memory.

The demonstration part of training includes stating the objective and showing the end results of the process. The trainer provides a step-by-step demonstration of the process while the trainee reads the written procedure aloud. The trainee highlights key points of the process, such as safety or quality issues.

After the demonstration, the trainee performs the process from memory, repeating the key points of the process. The trainer assists the trainee as necessary to perform the process as defined in the written procedure.

After the initial demonstration and trial run, the training may need to be repeated multiple times until the trainee reaches a satisfactory level of proficiency.

Improving Training Compliance

An obsolete procedure or one that is not being followed is traditionally viewed as a training issue. Increasing process compliance requires a comprehensive solution including a documentation system that can swiftly process document changes.

Conducting follow-up training sessions will ensure process compliance. The trainer reinforces the importance of the key points of the procedure and will also discover potential improvements to the written procedure.

Training Matrix

A training matrix identifies all team members and lists the available job procedures. It identifies the training requirements and training status of each person. A simple training matrix is shown below:

Name	Job 1	Job 2	Job 3	Job 4	Job 5
Joe S.	O	O	*	*	*
Jane A.	*	OK	O	OK	*
Ted O.					OK
Sara C.	OK	OK	O	OK	O

Legend: *   Target item for training

       O   On-the-job training

       OK   Proficient

Machines

Current and new equipment must be validated to determine its capabilities and limitations. Analyzing part-to-part inspection data over an extended time can provide insights into the capability and limitations of the equipment. The complexity of the validation process is determined by the criticality of the machine.

Equipment manufacturers provide maintenance schedules to maintain consistent performance. In addition, every organization should develop a series of routine maintenance procedures that will cover end-of-job maintenance; end-of-shift maintenance; end-of-day maintenance; and weekly, monthly, quarterly, and annual maintenance.

Improper machine setup can cause intermittent defects and slowly destroy a piece of equipment. Thus, a setup procedure should be developed to verify each machine's effectiveness at producing parts, throughout the entire production lot.

It helps greatly to make visible markings or gradiations to assist in performing setup and adjustments. The photograph below shows a pointer to indicate setup specification. When all machine adjustments are metered, a setup specification checklist may replace a setup work instruction.

Statistical Process Control (SPC) may be needed to monitor machine performance over a period of time. For critical part quality specifications, frequent inspections may be required to determine if a machine setting needs to be adjusted.

Materials

Consistency of material specifications does wonders to process stability and predictability. All components, parts, and materials must have specifications and acceptable tolerances, including cosmetic or visual standards.

Delivery specifications such as packaging requirements and lead times should also be established to ensure that materials arrive undamaged and on time.

A computer-based inventory system such as materials-requirement planning (MRP) or enterprise-resource planning (ERP) does not cover all types of materials. These systems often focus on high-cost or bulky items.

A simple visual inventory-management system can help in managing items not covered by MRP-ERP. A simple manual inventory system, called kanban, can be deployed to supplement an MRP-ERP systems to improve process compliance.

Once material specifications are on hand, suppliers must fully understand the requirements. A supplier-management process from the purchasing and quality departments can provide objective feedback for suppliers to use in ensuring compliance and implementing improvements.

Methods

Workplace procedures are typically classified by (1) company, (2) department, and (3) job. In addition, a process map can provide a visual representation of how the organization works from start to finish.

A flow diagram should be used, starting with the big-picture view and progressing down to the department level. In addition, a list of main steps, key points, and responsibility can provide more details.

Example of a Procedure Format

Instructions	Main Step	Key Points

Below is a simple example of a process map.

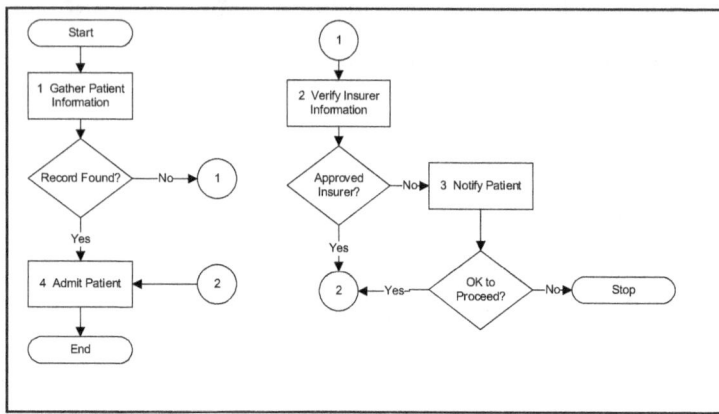

An example format is shown below for main steps, key points, and responsibility.

Main Step	Key Points	Responsibility
1. Gather patient information	• Form DSH-143	Preadmittance
2. Verify insurer information	• Document authorization code • Identify discrepancies	Preadmittance
3. Notify patient	• Identify discrepancies • Provide payment options	Customer service
4. Admit patient	• Enter patient info • Verify diagnosis code • Enter treatment code	Admittance

Data

Data should be treated like raw material. It has to be complete, accurate, and delivered on time. The first set of data is called the *product-service master record*. This contains the specifications and data required to build a product or perform a service, such as specifications, procedures, guidelines, engineering drawings, and photo examples.

Whenever a product is built or a service delivered, data is collected on a product-service history record. In the manufacturing environment, this is known as the *batch record* or *lot record*. In the service environment, it is called, simply, a *service record*. It contains specifications such as work-center number, names, dates, settings, materials used, quantity produced, scrap materials, and quality-inspection records.

Focus on Compliance

Step-by-Step Procedures
Focus on Compliance

Creating a Training System

Instructions

1. Define the purpose of the training system.

2. Choose a procedure format.

3. Create the cover page for the procedure. This includes background information about the process, such as approvals, required materials, and defects prevented.

4. Write a procedure for how to document the current process using work instruction forms and a cover page.

5. Write a procedure for how to route a procedure for feedback and approval.

6. Write a procedure for how to conduct training and improve process compliance.

7. Write a procedure for how to revise a procedure.

8. Train team members.

9. Schedule time for writing procedures and training employees. Use downtime, changeover, breaks, overtime, and the like.

10. Post a procedure-writing to-do list on the team board.

11. Post a training matrix on the team board.

Writing a Work Instruction

Instructions

1. Select a process to document.

2. Select a partner to help you develop the procedure.

3. Go to the location of the actual process.

4. Assign one person to perform the process proficiently and the other to write the instructions legibly.

5. Perform the actual process step by step. Do not modify or improve the current method. Submit process improvements to the team for feedback and approval.

6. Write one instruction for each action step. Include all specifications and critical information within each instruction.

7. Avoid using "and" and "then" to connect multiple instruction. Use "and" only for multiple subjects.

8. Write instructions to complete the process effectively. Leave one blank line between instructions so details can be added later.

9. Write down all instructions necessary to complete the process.

10. Group the instructions into main steps that complete a specific objective or subassembly.

11. Choose a representative verb and subject from within each group of instructions to identify each main step.

12. Write each main step in line with the first instruction of each group.

13. Complete all main steps for the entire process.

14. Identify reference points, directions, specifications, and critical items within each main step.

15. List these items as key points, starting with the main step.

16. Complete key points for all main steps.

17. Draw figures and illustrations for the procedure. Use diagrams, pictures, and flowcharts.

18. Complete the cover page.

19. Review all forms for spelling and legibility.

20. Sign the cover page to indicate your approval.

Example of a Procedure Format

Instructions	Main Step	Key Points

Routing a Procedure for Approval

Instructions

1. Give the completed procedure to knowledgeable team members for review and feedback.

2. Revise the procedure until a consistent team standard is identified.

3. Route the procedure to the support staff for feedback and approval, and revise the procedure to include any support-staff changes.

4. Route the procedure through quality assurance, if necessary.

5. Assign a control number, and indicate the initial revision level.

6. Store one official copy of the procedure in the team area.

7. Archive the original procedure for safekeeping.

8. Add the procedure to the team's training matrix.

Training Procedure

Instructions

1. Schedule time for training at the location of the actual process.

2. Show the end result of the process to the trainee.

3. Review the procedure cover page for background information.

4. Perform the process while the trainee reads the procedure aloud.

5. Assist the trainee as he or she performs the process from memory while verbalizing the main steps and key points.

6. Repeat the training cycle as necessary.

7. Ensure that the trainee can perform the entire process from memory and accurately verbalize all main steps and key points.

Improving Procedure Compliance

Instructions

1. Go to the work center where the process will be performed.

2. Greet the trainee, and indicate your desire to follow up on the previous training and to capture any process improvements he or she may have discovered.

3. Watch the trainee perform the process.

4. Ensure that the trainee completes each main step and is aware of all the key points of the process.

5. Discuss differences between the written procedure and the process being performed by the trainee.

6. Submit process improvements to the team for feedback and approval. Update the procedure as necessary.

7. Retrain or coach the trainee on any process changes.

8. Encourage the trainee to perform the process according to the procedure.

9. Update the team's training matrix.

10. Repeat follow-up training sessions until the trainee is proficient.

Revising a Procedure

Instructions

1. Submit process improvements to the teams and support staff for feedback and approval.

2. Send or give the revised procedure to knowledgeable team members for review and feedback.

3. Revise the procedure until a new team standard has been identified.

4. Route the procedure to the support staff for feedback and approval, and revise the procedure to reflect any support-staff changes.

5. Route the revised procedure through quality assurance, if necessary.

6. Revise the original copy of the procedure, and assign the next revision level.

7. Update the copy of the procedure in the team area. Discard any obsolete procedures distributed in the work area.

8. Archive the old version to maintain a revision history.

9. Update the team's training matrix to indicate that the process has been changed and that training is necessary.

Chapter 4: Managing Improvements

Constant Focus on Process Compliance

Full compliance to process and performance standards ensures process stability and predictability. Process noncompliance produce product defects, inferior customer service, and customer complaints. The nonconformance reporting (NCR) process in a quality system tackles systemic issues, while the issue-resolution process is a proactive step toward resolving issues or concerns that slow down the team or stop it from performing to its fullest capacity.

Performance Data

Setting up an issue-resolution process is simple. Create a log to document each issue, and add the following details:

- Issue noted by
- Issue date
- Resolved date
- Notes

Issue-Resolution Scorecard

A performance scorecard encourages the identification of issues. It also shows overall performance and effectiveness of the team and technical-support structure.

The scorecard shows the following data:

1. Issues identified
2. Issues resolved
3. Issues open
4. Oldest open issue

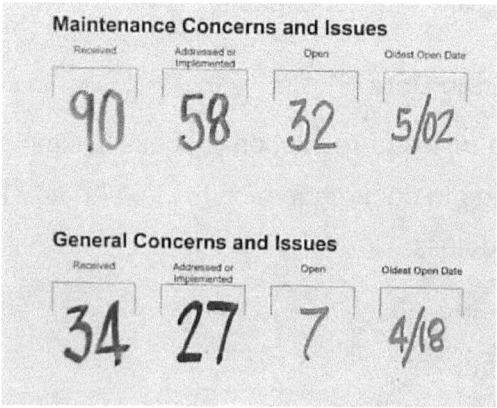

Maintenance Concerns and Issues

Received	Addressed or Implemented	Open	Oldest Open Date
90	58	32	5/02

General Concerns and Issues

Received	Addressed or Implemented	Open	Oldest Open Date
34	27	7	4/18

Employee Suggestion System

A robust suggestion system should be implemented only after launching the issue-resolution process. A suggestion system is focused on improving systems and procedures, while an issue-resolution process is focused on resolving system noncompliance.

An effective and robust suggestion system requires swift review, implementation, and feedback. Establishing a transparent and visible process encourages employees to actively participate in suggesting and implementing improvements. Posting a scorecard on the number of items identified, the number of implemented suggestions, and the number of open items is simple and effective.

Setting Up the Rules of the Game

Suggestions need to be encouraged to improve safety, quality, delivery, and cost. These factors define the scope of a valid employee suggestion.

Developing a simple process-flow diagram for processing suggestions will make the process transparent and visible to all team members.

Implementation

Before introducing the suggestion system, the work area should be prepared. This includes posting a suggestion flow chart and designating an area to log suggestions.

Procedures and guidelines need to be developed to define the acceptance criteria and implementation process. In addition, the work team's scope, responsibility, and budget need to be defined. Suggestions that require implementation beyond the capabilities and scope of the work team should be escalated to the support staff. It is therefore important for the support staff to be trained and ready before launching a suggestion system.

To swiftly process and respond to suggestions, the operational work teams will validate and implement majority of the suggestions. The work team should have all required resources, such as a budget and time to implement suggestions.

Recognition and Reward

Traditional monetary rewards for employee participation are detrimental to teamwork and can be highly discouraging. Team luncheons or awards recognizing the entire team is an effective approach to reinforce collective team effort and process compliance.

The issue-resolution process and the suggestion system are tools to help operational teams and the support staff achieve performance objectives. The employee recognition and reward system may be embedded in the JPR system.

Managing Improvements

Step-by-Step Procedures
Managing Improvements

Tracking Resolution of Issues

Instructions

1. Create an issue log documenting the following:

   - Issue number

   - Description

   - Submitted by

   - Date submitted

   - Resolution notes

   - Resolution date

   - Resolved by

2. Create the scorecard. It should be printed on cardstock and laminated. The scorecard should document the following:

   - Number of issues received

   - Number of issues resolved

   - Number of open issues

   - Date of oldest open issue

3. Hang the issue log in the team meeting area.

4. Train the team to log issues as they observe them.

5. Validate new entries during the team meeting.

6. Decide on the action plan. Set up a problem-solving session, if necessary.

7. Assign team members to resolve the issue.

8. Direct out-of-scope issues to the support staff.

9. Update the scorecard once a week.

Submitting a Suggestion for Improvement

Instructions

1. Develop a suggestion that improves safety, quality, delivery, or cost.

2. Ensure that the suggestion is within the suggestion parameters.

3. Get a blank suggestion form from the team meeting area.

4. Fill out name, date, and team name.

5. Describe the current situation, and illustrate as necessary. Include data and specific details.

6. Describe the proposed suggestion, and illustrate as necessary. Include as much detail as possible, and attach supporting documents.

7. Indicate improvements between the current situation and the proposed suggestion. Use data, and be specific.

8. Present the suggestion to the team during the team meeting.

9. Validate new items in the team meeting. Any new item must improve safety, quality, delivery, or cost and be within the expense budget.

10. Help the contributor modify the suggestion to make it valid, if necessary.

11. Determine whether the team can implement the approved suggestion.

12. Route the approved suggestion to management-support staff, if necessary.

Routing a Suggestion to the Support Staff

Instructions

1. Present the team-approved suggestion during the support-staff meeting.

2. Ensure that the suggestion is valid. A valid suggestion will improve safety, quality, delivery, or cost and be within the expense budget.

3. Decide whether to implement the suggestion.

4. Provide the team leader with an answer quickly. Choose a maximum target response time, such as two weeks. If a suggestion is rejected, explain the reason(s) for the rejection.

6. Create an action-item log.

7. Implement the suggestion as soon as possible. Choose a maximum target implementation time, such as two months.

8. Write the implementation date and number on the suggestion log.

9. Update the suggestion chart on the team board.

10. File the suggestion forms in chronological order.

Chapter 5: Workplace Organization

Creating the Image That Sets the Standards

An organization's image delivers a clear message about how a company operates. An organization's marketing literature goes through an elaborate process of graphic design and presentation to communicate standards of excellence. Similarly, a company's physical environment communicates its standards of excellence and performance.

Workplace organization defines the culture and work ethic of a company. It also defines the standards regarding how people function and present themselves. Contract workers and visitors will immediately recognize and adapt to these standards.

It is recommended that an organization implement the Five Basics of Workplace Organization prior to any process-improvement initiative. Successful implementation of the Five Basics of Workplace Organization will provide a boost in employee morale, highlight nonconformances, identify scrap-generating issues, lower inventory, and improve efficiency.

The Five Basics of Workplace Organization

Below is a rendition of workplace organization introduced as part of the Toyota Production System. The Five Basics of Workplace Organization are as follows:

Five Basics	Description
Cleanliness	Keep work area clean, spotless, or pure. Keep area clear of scrap and dirt. Maintain cleanliness of tools, fixtures, and equipment exterior. Remove items not related to the work activity. Designate an area for personal effects.
Orderliness	Keep work area orderly, organized, or methodical. Designate a place for tools and materials. Label and identify area of intended contents. Develop a process to communicate material replenishment or oversupply.
Tidiness	Keep work area neat and compact. Design the most practical and efficient work area. Lay out materials and scrap to flow into

designated holding areas. Maintain the least amount of material inventory in the work area. Move frequently used tools and materials closer to the point of use.

Process   Define the areas of responsibility. List the expectations, and create a compliance checklist. Define the survey frequency, and conduct a baseline survey. Conduct training, and provide the tools and materials to accomplish the expectations. Conduct routine surveys.

Discipline   Communicate the importance of process compliance to achieve performance standards. Develop a set of performance metrics for the entire company, for each department, and for each team. Integrate 5S as part of the performance-review process.

Implementation

A well-defined audit checklist establishes standards and dictates the level of success at implementing an effective workplace-organization campaign.

The five-step implementation process is as follows:

1. **Define areas of responsibilities**. Get a floor plan of your building or space, and divide the area for each team. Allocate common aisleways to teams so that the entire layout of the building is assigned to a specific team.

2. **Create a checklist of standards**. Create a simple audit checklist that defines expectations or standards. Performance should be measured by the number of compliant items on the checklist.

3. **Provide performance feedback**. Conduct routine (monthly) audits. Discuss the audit results with the team. Encourage the team to improve the score at least one point per month.

4. **Post the performance scorecard**. Create a simple scorecard showing the number of

compliant items in the checklist. Chart the progress monthly.

5. **Provide resources to implement workplace organization**. Provide the necessary tools and equipment required for the team to improve the 5S audit.

Manufacturing Five Basics Audit Checklist

Here is an example checklist for manufacturing.

Cleanliness		Yes	No
1.	Area is free of scrap, litter, and dirt.		
2.	Irrelevant items are not stored in the area.		
3.	Trash and scrap containers are emptied before overflowing.		
4.	Postings are relevant and up to date.		
5.	Equipment exterior and paint finish appears clean.		
6.	Tools and fixtures are kept clean.		
7.	Floor marking appears clean and clearly defines the work area.		

Orderliness		Yes	No
8.	Aisleways are clearly defined by floor tape or paint.		
9.	Aisleways and safety equipment are clear from any obstruction.		
10.	Materials, equipment, and fixtures have designated areas.		
11.	Designated areas clearly identify inspection and test status.		
12.	Designated areas are labeled to indicate their intended contents.		
13.	Items are maintained within the designated area.		
14.	Materials are not leaning against walls, pillars, or equipment.		
15.	The tool and fixture area is organized and labeled.		
16.	Personal items are consolidated in a designated area.		

Tidiness | Yes | No

		Yes	No
17.	Materials are stacked neatly, and postings are mounted squarely.		
18.	Frequently used materials, tools, and fixtures are located close to the point of use.		
19	Materials, procedures, and tools are easily accessible.		

Process | Yes | No

		Yes	No
20.	Sufficient cleaning tools and supplies are provided to the work area.		
21.	The storage area for cleaning tools and supplies is clean and organized.		
22.	Procedures are written for routine cleaning and maintenance.		
23.	The training log verifies training of team members.		

Discipline | Yes | No

		Yes	No
24.	The Five Basics review is conducted routinely.		
25.	Scorecards or charts provide feedback to team members.		

Office Five Basics Audit Checklist

Below is an example checklist for the office environment.

Cleanliness		Yes	No
1.	Area is free of scrap, litter, and dirt.		
2.	Irrelevant items are not stored in the area.		
3.	Trash and scrap containers are emptied before overflowing.		
4.	Postings are relevant and up to date.		
5.	Work stations and office equipment exteriors are clean.		
6.	Materials are not stored behind furniture and storage cabinets.		

Orderliness		Yes	No
7.	Office layout provides easy access to each workstation.		
8.	Aisleways, circuit breakers, emergency exits, and other safety equipment are clear of any obstruction.		
9.	Documents and materials have designated inbound, in-process, outbound, and storage locations.		
10	Nonconforming and sample materials are labeled.		
11.	Binders, folders, and containers are labeled with their intended contents.		
12.	Items are maintained within the designated area.		
13.	Materials are not leaning against walls, pillars, or office equipment.		

14.	Power cords and cables are kept out of sight.	
15.	Business-use postings are limited to a designated area.	
16.	Personal effects are limited to a designated area.	

Tidiness	**Yes**	**No**
17.	Binders, folders, containers, and materials are neatly stored.	
18.	Postings are mounted squarely and appear organized.	
19.	Reminder notes are neat and tidy and do not dominate the work center.	

Process	**Yes**	**No**
20.	If a cleaning service is not provided, sufficient cleaning tools and supplies area provided to the work area.	
21.	The storage area for cleaning tools and supplies is clean and orderly.	

Discipline	**Yes**	**No**
22.	Guidelines are documented for maintaining a clean and organized work area.	
23.	The training log verifies training of team members.	
24.	The Five Basics review is conducted routinely.	
25.	A scorecard or chart provides feedback to team members.	

Step-by-Step Procedures
Workplace Organization

Assigning Areas of Responsibility

Instructions

1. Post a laminated map of the department in the support-staff meeting room.

2. Draw the department boundary with the support staff's help.

3. Split the department into areas of team responsibility. Label each team area on the map.

4. Conduct an initial Five Basics survey of each team area. The entire support staff should walk around for this initial survey.

5. Indicate each team's score on the map.

6. Chart the average score of all the teams on the support-staff board.

7. Set a realistic goal for the department's average Five Basics score.

8. Draw the goal with a black horizontal line.

9. Create action plans with each team to raise each team's score one or two points per month.

10. Insert time into the production schedule for cleaning and organizing the workplace. Use downtime, changeover, breaks, overtime, and so on.

11. Acquire cleaning supplies.

Conducting the Five Basics Survey

Instructions

1. Conduct the survey with the team leader and supervisor on a regular schedule each month.

2. Record the team name, team leader's name, surveyor name, and date at the top of a blank survey form.

3. Walk through the team area, discussing positive and negative changes since the last survey.

4. Mark each category as a yes if it has been taken care of or a no if improvement is still required.

5. Note items that are out of place in the Notes section. Note praise, concerns, or suggestions in the margins.

6. Count the number of yeses as the survey score.

7. Post the survey on the team board, over the previous month's.

8. Update the Workplace Organization chart on the team board.

9. Review the survey at the next team meeting.

10. Review the survey scores and department average at the next support-staff meeting.

11. Use the suggestion process to improve the area.

Workplace Organization

Chapter 6: Effective Performance Reviews

The Job Performance Rveiew (JPR) system is designed to be data driven and objective and requires minimal effort for the supervisor. It has been field tested and implemented in various-sized companies and industries.

Design Considerations

The following factors were considered in the development of the JPR system:

- The performance measures for each job position must support the department goals.

- Performance data must be quick and easy to access.

- Performance standards must be clearly defined.

- It should take the supervisor no more than five minutes to gather the data and complete a JPR.

- The JPR session should take no more than ten minutes.

- The JPR ratings should be easily linked to wage adjustments or compensation models.

Rating System

Unlike traditional review systems, which use school-like grading systems, the JPR system uses a unique rating system. The starting point of the rating system is always at the Expected (5) level, and the data, being positive or negative, moves the rating to the set increments. The numerical ratings are provided in the chart below, and a description of each follows.

0	Change required
1 to 4	Contributing
5	Expected
6 to 9	Commendable
10	Exceptional

Change Required

The employee fails to deliver the expected performance. Performance-data documentation is required to support this rating. High levels of performance documentation are required. Performance reviews are given at a higher frequency, such as monthly or even weekly. Disciplinary action or even the warning process for termination is initiated.

Contributing

The employee performs below the standards of expectation. Performance-data documentation is required to support this rating. The supervisor may identify areas for improvement, begin the probationary process, or increase the review frequency.

Expected

The employee performs to standards or meets expected outcomes. This is the starting point of the rating scale. Use performance data to justify awarding a higher or lower rating. This is the only rating that does not require any performance documentation.

Commendable

The employee exceeds the expected levels of performance. Performance-data documentation is required to support this rating. He or she consistently goes beyond the performance standards on a month-to-month basis.

Exceptional

The employee consistently exceeds the established standards of performance on a year-to-year basis. This is a rare rating to award. Performance-data documentation is required to support this rating.

Components of a Job-Performance Review

Every JPR document will contain the following:

1. **List of performance measures**: A list of performance measures, the definition of each performance measure, and sources of data.

2. **Rating sheet:** A graduated scale of outcomes and the corresponding rating.

3. **Performance summary**: Rating of each performance item, noting the associated documentation to support the rating above and below the Expected (5) level.

Performance Measures

Performance measures are not limited to items that directly impact an individual. Total company, department, and team performance need to be considered.

Most performance measures are identified in the team meeting area. You can use some of the team performance measures and account for the individual impact of each item. Here is an example:

Defects Produced (1) Team
        (2) Individual

If team performance measures are not available, use the planning matrix to identify potential items.

	Input (supplier)	Process (team)	Output (finished product)
Safety	Hazardous material leaks	Accidents and near misses	Stack height compliance
Quality	Defects received	Defects produced	Defects shipped
Delivery	On-time delivery	Schedule compliance	On-time delivery
Cost	Purchase-price variance	Productivity	Purchase-price variance
Continuous Improvement	NCR-CAR	NCR-CAR Suggestions 5S score	NCR-CAR

Each performance measure must be clearly defined and must identify the source(s) of the data.

Also consider process-compliance and process-improvement items. Managers and supervisors can collect observations and use them as performance data.

Not all performance data is collected by an ERP-MRP or computer system. The supervisor may have to develop a performance data-collection form. If this is the case, every effort should be made to keep the form easy to use and submit it on a routine basis.

Example Performance Measures

Department and Company Performance Measures

1. On-Time Delivery
Definition: Product delivery to customer on or before the due date

Source of data: Monthly service-level report

2. Productivity
Definition: Total units produced per labor hour

Source of data: Shop-floor management data

3. Customer Feedback
Definition: Performance feedback from customers

Source of data: Customer feedback and customer incident reports

Individual Performance Measures

4. Internal Defects
Definition: Defects reported by rewind or folder-gluer operations

Source of data: Scrap form completed by finishing department

5. Productivity

Definition: Total shift good footage produced per labor hour

Source of data: Shop-floor management data

6. Compliance to Policy and Procedure

Definition: Compliance with corporate and department policies, guidelines, directives, and procedures

Source of data: Exceptional and substandard performance documented by the supervisor or manager

Performance Standards

Standards of performance can be gathered based on historical data or a cascade from the department goal. Make sure the goals are attainable.

Rating Sheet

A graduated scale of performance outcomes lists the appropriate rating for each item. This will make it easier for the supervisor to provide an objective and consistent rating. Here is an example:

Item	Outcome	Rating
Nonconformance reports (NCRs)	Additional NCRs	−1 for each
	2 NCRs	5
	0 NCRs	+1 for every quarter

Example JPR Rating Sheet

	Performance Standards	Value	Rating
1	On-time Delivery	100%	10
		99%	7
		98%	5
		97%	3
		96%	0

2	Department Productivity	2200	10
		1900	7
		1600	5
		1500	3
		1400	0

3	Customer Feedback	0	10
		5	7
		10	5
		15	3
		20	0

5	Internal Defects	3 Y with 0	10
		1 Y with 0	7
		3	5
		6	3
		9	0

6	Individual Productivity	See Machine Center Standards Sheet	10
			7
			5
			4 - 3
			0

7	Compliance with Policy & Procedure	++	10
		+	7
		0	5
		1 – 2 UO	4 - 3
		3 UO	0

Example Performance Summary

Name _____   JPR Review
                                  Period _____

	Rating	Weight	Score	Supporting Data
1. On-time Delivery		2		
2. Department Productivity		2		
3. Customer Feedback		1		
4. Internal Defects		1		
5. Individual Productivity		1		
6. Compliance with Policy & Procedure		1		
Sum of Column		8		
Overall JPR Rating				

Signatures

_____   _____   _____
Employee   Supervisor   HR Manager

Completing a JPR Form

Use the rating scale to reference the performance outcome and determine the JPR rating for each item. List supporting documents to justify a rating above or below the Expected (5) level. Write down any additional facts in the Notes section.

Calculate the total JPR rating for the period. Keep in mind that a rating of Expected (5) is a positive rating.

Review Process

Supervisors should realize that a JPR session is a historical review of performance data. The employee review should be scheduled for no more than ten minutes. Discussion regarding work issues or future job roles should be scheduled separately.

During the performance review, compare performance data with the set goals and objectives. In most cases, items that meet expectation (with a 5 rating) are discussed quickly. Items above and below the Expected (5) level will require a short discussion.

Linking JPR to Compensation

Translating an individual performance review into a numerical value provides the means for developing a compensation model for wage adjustments or bonuses.

In a wage-adjustment model, an organization develops a percentage distribution, as shown below:

Rating	Increase
7 and above	6%
6	5%
5	4%
4	3%
3 and below	0%

The distribution scale is applied to current employee wages in determining the total wage adjustments. The calculated total is compared to the budgeted amount, and the scale is adjusted up or down until the budgeted amount is matched.

Implementation

Implementation of a JPR system requires deliberate planning and execution. The implementation is a learning process for the entire company and requires patience from the supervisor and team members.

The implementation plan requires the supervisor and subordinates to develop the system jointly. This makes the JPR process transparent to the entire company and helps eliminate people's fear of JPRs.

Example Implementation Timetable

Week 1	Identify job positions
Week 2	Define performance measures
Week 3	Define rating worksheet
Week 4	Develop JPR documents
Week 5	Conduct employee overview
Weeks 6–8	Conduct first trial
Week 9	Review first trial
Weeks 9–12	Conduct second trial
Week 13	Review second trial
Weeks 14–17	Conduct third trial
Week 18	Review third trial
Week 19	Launch JPR systems

Step-by-Step Procedures
Effective Performance Reviews

JPR Implementation

Instructions

1. Define reporting relationships, referencing the organizational chart.

2. Define job positions.

3. Identify performance measures.

4. Define the source(s) of data.

5. Identify performance standards.

6. Develop a rating worksheet.

7. Develop the JPR form.

8. Conduct supervisor training.

9. Conduct employee training.

10. Conduct three monthly JPR trials.

JPR System Overview

Instructions

1. Conduct initial training.
2. Schedule start of review period.
3. Set up JPR filing system.
4. Document performance observations.
5. Complete JPR forms.
6. Submit JPR forms for review.
7. Update JPR forms.
8. Conduct individual reviews.
9. File JPR forms.

Completing a JPR Form

Instructions

1. Print JPR form.

2. Rate company and department JPR items.

3. Record company and department JPR items.

4. Copy a JPR form for each employee.

5. Rate individual JPR items.

6. Record individual items on JPR form.

7. Calculate total score.

8. Calculate overall JPR rating.

9. List supervisor notes.

10. Sign JPR forms.

11. Forward completed JPRs to HR or manager for validation.

Conclusion

As an operations manager, I always remind myself and the management-support staff not to micromanage operations. Our primary role is to develop systems and procedures for the entire organization to be self-powered, self-driven, and self-correcting. Developing the fundamental structure described in this book requires patience and persistence.

Take one small step at a time, and effectively implement each step by validating the process with all the people impacted by the process. Engage everyone, and tell them that this is a new process for you and for all of them. Also, request their patience and feedback on how to make this process work successfully.

As you implement each chapter of this book, I hope you see incremental process improvements, enhanced performance outcomes, and improved employee morale. Soon after the fundamental structure is in place, I highly recommend that you explore the implementation of process-improvement tools used in initiatives such as Lean Six Sigma, Total Quality Management, and the Toyota Production System.

Index

www.ingramcontent.com/pod-product-compliance
Lightning Source LLC
Chambersburg PA
CBHW051326170526
45166CB00002B/704